# THE MESSENGER

Winner of the Iowa Poetry Prize

# THE MESSENGER

by Stephanie Pippin

UNIVERSITY
OF IOWA PRESS
IOWA CITY

University of Iowa Press, Iowa City 52242
Copyright © 2013 by Stephanie Pippin
www.uiowapress.org
Printed in the United States of America

Design by Omega Clay

The University of Iowa Press is a member of Green
Press Initiative and is committed to preserving
natural resources.

Printed on acid-free paper

ISBN-13: 978-1-60938-164-6
ISBN-10: 1-60938-164-5
LCCN: 2012947366

For Andy

*Aimed at a distant bird, a flutter of white wings, he may feel—as it spreads out beneath him in a field of white— that he can never fail to strike. Everything he is has evolved to link the targeting eye to the striking talon.*

J. A. Baker

*We love the things we love for what they are.*

Robert Frost

# CONTENTS

## ACKNOWLEDGMENTS

Thanks to Garth Greenwell for your support, advice, and friendship.

Special thanks to Jennifer Bender, Susan Burkhardt, and Roger Wallace, for teaching me to handle and care for birds of prey.

I am grateful to my teachers Carl Phillips, Mary Jo Bang, and Mary Ellen Miller.

Grateful acknowledgement is made to the following journals in which these poems appeared: "Homecoming" and "Phaedra" in *Agni Online*; "Afterimage" in *Best New Poets 2010*.

# THE MESSENGER

# Afterimage

In Pompeii every girl is a fresco—
her right hand held in front of her stomach,
her left arm bent at the elbow.
Closed in her robe's smooth
volutes, she gives no hint of how
it must have sounded

so like the neighbors breaking
each other again. Song
of black-eye, song of fist.
Song of sometimes you make me
a little bit crazy, sometimes
you make me insane.

The lost are like this. Misheard,
slightly bent, a faint
assault on my dreaming.

It is perilous to be resilient
and a little sentimental.
It is enough to know
the clouds came down
on shuttered rooms. Then
the tremble, then the hush.

How can I be rid of these
swans painted on plaster,
this sky of promiscuous wings,
when I still see them
deckle edged and rolling with smoke.
Their jeweled eyes lamp the ash.

## The Messenger

Now that the sycamores branch off
into whiteness, they seem on the verge
of speech. This is the lesson
of grief, to listen to the chorus
at the water's edge, to read
the black weight of abandoned nests back
into portents of spring. Assemblage
of accidents, I gauge the distance
from my body to yours, my reflection gone
awry. I don't know where to lay
my wreath, my tribute. I tried
to make you mean my life, no

one without the other. I failed
to catch your message—that night—
the falling star, the laughing
children, my usual wringing of hands.
Your body took its meaning, spun
a knot of coldness and your small grave
opened. I turned my face away just then
and missed it.

# King Vulture

He too has a sense of humor. Wintering
indoors, waiting for his share
of gutted hare and my hand
to bring it, he practices his lunge, knows

how I wince. And his silver
eye beautifully evolved, and his jaw—
I am sorry for these small
creatures that come to me dead;

even as I clean them I turn their heads
away. I do not want the knife
or the smell of their blood.
But necessity

speaks to me, angel stinking of his own
excitement. His wings thrash
air with the sound of tearing cloth.
How he wants me

now
coming closer to look in my face
and see himself looking back.
The rest is routine: I

defend myself as he feigns to eat me.
This is love. He sees straight
to my heart and is still. We play dead.
All that is still is dead.

# January

The water is blue-black then
silver by noon. The snow
has started. After we clear
the doe of her heart
and lungs, after we pour her insides out
in a bucket, I find her hollow
shape is the form I want
to sink into, pushing
my limbs into hers, running for her
life through the valley—
its grasses and pines, its lake and the
circling of dihedral wings.
Theirs is the mind
I've tried to fall through, their alien
strangeness. Only here
in the grass is my real
self—mammal-solid, her wide
eyes cooling in her head.
And the body
that says I will never
fly. If I could I would love her
harder, would slip
through the door of her ribcage
into a new life—my head
on her shoulders, my legs gone
loose and airy for leaping—the old
trick of a body transformed.

## Meteor Shower Peaks

Double cluster, the Perseid radiant, night
and a telescope looks over
the heads of rescuers bent listening
at a narrow hole drilled
into the sandstone
earth. No air,
no voice, no living
men, only the night
sky of falling

debris, and grown men crying as children
gape at the stars. Like Gilgamesh
for his heart's
brother, these men weep as they reach
now only for bodies. The stars fall
and are silent on the horizon, but O sweet
young men of Utah, when the earth
speaks, it speaks of you.

# Dwelling

Hunger made her reckless,
Made her covet the garden
In spite of its thorns.

The red fruit, with its buds
Like a string of little time bombs,
Had forgotten her: pregnant, her fur

Almost gray in the semidarkness,
And the strangeness of her
Own body, fat with urges—

Now starving, now sick.
And still the fruit would not drop.
Then, as if conjured, an owl.

The grass writhes as she flees
Her bed of tiny mice. There is blood
Enough to go around.

It is all they will know: her
Comings and goings, the brief,
Hot milk, her tongue. In the end,

She may eat them, too.
This is how to love the earth:
Like a hand

Passing blindly, finger
By finger, through the soil
And stink of leaves.

To crawl toward the smell of warm fur.

# The Dove

The weight of this
is more than you imagined.
Not a small pear in your palm,
beating.

Or a pearl, ripe
to be pried from the green
throat of an elm.
It shines and shines.

A dead thing never
looked so sweet, dry
ink of an eye, wing
like a stopped voice.

You lift it, the empty
husk of a message,
not knowing what it means.
I know what it means.

## Morning

A bird is loose in the room. I am thinking
of accidents of timing, the slightest change
in a body as final. I speak of need, meaning
panic. Outside, the grip of winter thins.
Outside, the thickening trees.

What I can't understand is the hold
this has on me: that it will hit and fall
eventually, that after the bird is down, my
mind will confuse its pain with my own.

## Tether

The thread of your blood—thin
silk suddenly knotted.
I cheat—

loving the hawk, her talons
through my glove,
my vein standing purple

attention. The clamp
of that foot, the sport.
Messy affection

gaudy as blisters, winter's
blood clock counting
mice or pigeons

at the base of an oak. Shiverers!
And this one—
released then reeling me

home to her.
All that I've seen is emptied
from me like Judgement.

I am divisible from the mindless
grip of this world
where your tiny body burst—

your blood rare red as columbine your
breath released as relic—
from your feathers turned

ash in my hands.

# The Kill

It is spring before the owls hatch, the ground
is hard, the day sky white at noon. White,

everything white. Such a clean place to die.
In the air, a chill, a chattering of bird-angst,

and the hum of green flies, satisfied, as if it is
kindness that spreads them over the doe.

When they move her body seems to move.
When they scatter I think she wants me

to see her. I look away and hear the sound
that was her breathing.

# Stork

Even clipped, his wing
has its redeeming quality. Black
and then white, his feathers
are holy things, lifted for relief.

The sky shrinks from him.

I, too, am beyond his reach
though we occupy the same
space in the small
hours of traveling loss.

It is sudden. From the dim
corner, his head.
Annunciatory gesture
pale as the angel's sleight of hand.

# Hatch

Held to my ear the egg clicks,
then chirps and is
silent. The air sac
has drawn down.
The hours from pip
to hatch, days
to trace the breaks, to see
the shell breached,
are agony.
It is hard to give birth
to yourself. Egg-
tooth, then beak,
then the whole
bird emerges. Removed
to the brooder she is
too new—it hurts to see her
damp and matted,
how she trembles. In the morning
I will unfold her
foot; touch each little
point of her talons—
already sharp
to draw blood.

## Open Season

Having starved for months, the fox
means business.
She is wisp-thin and serious,

following marks indelible
as lines on an open palm that sing
rabbit, rabbit.

Her world has narrowed down
to what she leaves behind.
Given the chance

I would side with her heart,
its terrific kick and the hot
taste of survival,

but this is a matter of motherhood.
In their warren rabbits cringe,
some abort their young,

and I remember what it meant
to want. Hunger
was the spot where a pulse

leapt up to meet the tongue.

## Lake

They've pushed out the eggs that wait
to be broken, that now are broken. Unceasing

thrill of their throats as they take in the air open-
mouthed as they fall, and when they fall

I fold them into my palm with my fingers,
the waste of them wet in my hand.


The water stands black under those bodies
that skim and don't drown. Taught

by design to turn, as they turn
they disappear. Where light

strikes the water's surface, I wait to be broken,
looking for wings where there are none.

# Lone Elk

1

RUMINANTS

Full beauty of the herd—
gold-brown, glowing
in the grassy bottomlands,
browsing the asters,
coralberry, acorns. Let wild
in the forest, we
multiplied, cows
fat with mothering, all of us
a single mind, precise
as the universe. Before
the war, before the army
fence cuts us
off from food and movement,
there are so many trees,
a forest thickened by clear
cutting—trees that carry
sound in their branches
like the voices of elk. Our voices.

2

CALVING SEASON

Our last spring, starving.
And the calves
come anyway. Browsing,
we strip the trees, clear
the grassland and then
there is nothing to eat.
The trucks come
and go and no one
feeds us, though they smell
like food. Our milk dries up.
Tenacity will keep us
suckling into summer,
searching out the last
grasses, ignorant
that what comes for us
is here already. The ground
unfreezes where they bury
their weapons.
We graze there too.

## 3

It is a kindness to shoot them.
One charged our truck. Rage
of a dying bull, a noise
so terrible it takes the breath,
cannot be spoken of later.
Men make sport
of it. We hunt the suffering
herd where they are
already dying, bounded
by fences. Even in their weakness
it is slow going. Winter
helps us cull the rest
until only the old
bulls are left and those
so slow the trees cannot
cover them.

Ungutted, minus the blood loss,
the weight
of the dead is the same
as the weight of the living.
More than a hundred
altogether. Their increase
steady, a watch set ticking.
The bodies are processed, sent
to feed hospitals. We keep the heads,
the ovaries, the stomachs.
We make notes.
As if there were a future,
we plan habitat.
On a table the skull
of a yearling reaches
maturity. We remember
the herd in our work.
They have vanished, they
will reappear—a jawbone,
the branch of a spine.

5

Silence, the hush
of trees in the rain. It is nearly
spring again. The men
go on burying
munitions; the deer
graze the forest. Now the trees
are harrowing trees.
They would speak. They have
a stench like standing water.
In the forest nothing
moves but oak
branches. The war
winds down, the soldiers'
days are numbered.
Still they stop on every
path to look for tracks.
Asters rise
like steam from the grass.
A thousand eyes are opening.

6

For you the children
bring their dimes to school.
Survivor of five
months of slaughter, then
years alone in trees
grown thick with horror.
How you managed,
scavenging
among deer and vultures,
is anyone's guess. Your terror
at being found, incalculable.
Your existence, inexplicable—
a hellish magnificence,
a message
from the dead. Or just
a lonely animal.
When the others come you unwind
yourself from the trees.

## Red Pines

*Calm*, I say, and bring my glove beneath her
feet, urge the unnatural
step to my arm.

Above us in bonewhite
branches of sky, the pines
hold their clusters. The blight

has not reached them yet, these
needles from the moon's
eye, cold and

unyielding through late frost.
I cannot keep my mind from her. Urgent,
her wings lift with my steps, jesses

straining as she leans for release—
the slip from my wrist, the shriek
in the grass.

She cannot live without plunder.
Bundle of nerves
and blood and sustenance, the egg

is its own law and more real than I, more
alive—a galaxy her wings obey
in everything they do.

# Brazil, 1832

*after Charles Darwin*

*I have seen a little boy,*

The slightest modification
Of waves carries strangers
To shore.

*six or seven years old,*

Why must I unearth
What comes to me anyway
Eventually?

*struck thrice with a horse-whip*

I remember my mother's hat
Was something
Killed for its feathers.

*(before I could interfere)*

Let the children come
Unto me knowing nothing
Of science or kindness.

*on his naked head,*

When I wake I should remember
Nothing that happened,
But think myself a flower.

*for having handed me a glass*

The waves in their gray
Ruches remind me
Of tormented pigeons.

*of water not quite clean.*

At night I am cut
Free. I confuse myself
With birds.

# The Peregrine

Cast into the white
amnesia of clouds
he leaves this ground
delighted; disappears
above the lift
of pigeons. It is stunning—
their wings synched
to an internal
pattern of panic
and the speck of him
above, black
spot moving in and out
of sun. Why
do they drive themselves
into the open
space of the field?
I try to see them
as he sees them—a surface
disturbance, the flock
that flies as one
body, blind
in the light, knowing
one among many is no loss at all.

## A Nest

A ground nest—
its three eggs crushed.

After the fact
I can only imagine
what it was

as the quail
comical, large
onion with plumage
sets her eye horribly
on me.

She cannot conceive
the difference between us.

# Diving Horse

His body is pure screen for the eye
to build its miracles. So many
entertainments, I can set my watch
by his dive, by his ridiculous
descent from the high platform.

No one loves him enough
to botch the drop.
They let him hurt
as children hurt, certain
only of the present world.

Hell is the blank blue yawn
of the tank at the end of the dive.
Hell is the ground that flattens him out.

He is innocent in his hope.
Even after a hundred times
his legs push
against the tilt that drops him.

I love him as I love everything
human that makes me want to fall
and be delivered
headfirst into darkness.

# Homecoming

I thought I was dreaming him—
man in the hallway, a husband, a leopard.
*A leopard altering light.* And the smell
of him, sweet like rot
deep in a tree. Then he dropped his bags.

That morning I cut
across the neighbor's field
on my way to the store. Movement where
there should be none—a dead hare
animated by maggots, beetles puppeting
its body. I almost
put my foot on the snake. Rat snake
streaking out, away from me deeper
into wet grass. The thrill—
visceral. Of my nature.

He sleeps. He is dreaming
children in a phalanx of vultures, their dead
wings hum in his chest when I lay
my ear to it—ragged
gutturals of breath, chest
where the starving
swarm.

Soup cans, cantaloupe ask
what is normal. A woman's head
floats up over tabloids.
She wants to know did he come back
different?

*He came home with bullets for teeth.*
He came home made of glittering
rock from the riverbeds, the marrow
of what happened there. He came home
a Protean con man, folding
and unfolding like paper—

now lover, now leopard, now swan.

## Shiloh

The shadows of boys move, hunched like animals in the grass under low clouds. They know the territory, its thistles and occasional jays. They know where they buried the dog. Whatever they find is authentic treasure—sometimes a bullet in shallow ground, sometimes a button. The cats have been here too. There is the smell of fur and urine, a thread of blood. Rain and after the rain, no light. Leaves make a dark song out of wind. At the field's edge, a delicate clatter of hooves. The boys listen, quivering like rabbits. The earth is frightening: immense and very old.

# Iron Bridge

Thinking luck
follows luck I
turn my face away
from the spring
mallards that move
through the underworld
murk of the bridge's shadow—
green gleams in black
water, a message, my
letter from hell.
I turn from their eggs
toward the reeds still
strung with last
fall's milkweed
silk clinging unviable
to the brittle pods.
Halfway across, pain—
fish-slick, a fast
rabbit, a thread
of blood singing
last chance, last
chance.
So she goes—
my mermaid, a blade
of grass—unknown.
On the other side,
a meadow. My body
has changed its ways.
I can speak
to the dead now,
to what
the dead intend.

# Raven

She needs work. July
rots around us; stargazer
lilies wilt like angels
overthrown, a bed of throats
collapsing. I tell her

stories as my fingers preen
the gloss of feathers—
a girl's head among apples, a father
eats his own child. The child
comes singing itself

back to the world, each
note barbed
black as trees and wound
into music. Why do I care

if they die?
These flowers—their faces
wasted but rapt
and busy with insects,
their yellow lights—follow me

into the dry smell of wood and
pea gravel. I barehand the bird
to her perch. I am afraid
her trust is temporary, that the world

in which she
cannot live, cannot save herself,
is the world she will want

eventually. And I
the cage that keeps her from it.

## Phaedra

Nights the stars twitch like nerves.
Those skies are like her, dead
and not dead, and the sea—
Listen

she fell in love like a lunatic.
Like a goat she would have eaten
all his clothes to see him
walk away naked.

# Gone

On the road where the barn and its stone
walls erode ship-like
listing toward its northeast
corner, three coyote cross and pause
to look at me. I am so close to the late-spring
stink of them I can see one nearly
drags her teats in the dust. I too
have left the young behind me—
a den of possibility

abandoned. I feel the sting of it.
And a confusion of my body
that tugs me to follow
their vanishing shapes. What they fear,
I fear: extinction, the kick of a deer, the mewl
of hungry pups, and myself
hunted and cornered and bloody.
This is the line they cannot cross. I
am their catastrophe. I am lost
when they melt into the crippled
wilderness of farm fields.

## Riverlands

In the time it takes to recognize
dead as dead I've stepped on an egret
(long cross of its body, wings
spread; even grounded it flies)
and withdrawn, repulsed by the softness of it
all. All this Missouri
ground—open, sogged with August,
morels swelling like lungs
in the muck, and the bird barely
touched. Its eyes are gone.

Remember how I tried to make you fly?
Motion in frost where the bees hived
at the field's other side—a rabbit's bewildered
leap in air and you, unhooded, taking
your time. A great
patience, and a fear of you
not returning to my glove. Your heavy eye,
your sight, was the straight
line that taught me what isn't dead
is dying. You are gone weeks

ago, released to the season, belonging
to yourself. I return, mother
enough to know the elastic
band that keeps me circling
the ground is love. The egret,
still shining its whites, stares with nothing
at nothing. Every wheeling
shadow is your shadow. My mistake
was believing I taught you
to kill. I taught you to return.

## What I Wanted

from the unwound, sticky hibiscus
you loved so much you could cry:

a hallelujah chorus, a eureka of finches,
startling even to the edge of the lawn.

What would we be without this
velvet largess? Where would we go

when we die? Even now you have half-
slipped into its cup. I see you there,

nodding in pollen, then remember
it is not you. The flower took you,

when you stalled, and closed like a throat.
Now it holds you, weeping, up to me.

# Hero

I am handsome when I dream.

I was made for such animal glory,
horrible and ordinary, a kept lion
that, reverting,
will turn and kill the herd.

Sleep is the heat going out of me. Arterial
hymn of my other self: a bat that hibernates
by freezing solid.

                                      Someone dead
who has not died. My wing,
not the same as a wing,
but what the wing became as it chose
to stay unbeautiful:

wrist  palm  finger  claw.  Whatever hunts

to feed its young, then leaves these bones
for me to think about,

                                       will circle back
ill wind, will find in the wide, wet
eye of the bull,
disbelief, and the blood behind it.

*And he sang he would tear her to pieces*

Dark in mind and
untranslatable,
the man she staggered after
went on

turning himself one shape
then another:
crocodile, leopard.
Imagine

his heart electric,
unsentimental
as hunger is
until given the slip.
Only then the grief: his

like any other and hers
a gazelle's head
buried in reeds, rabbit
the dogs run for.

# Florida

His yield has a bladder
like a lady's clutch purse. Silver
and glistening,
it gradually loses its heat.

He exclaims eggs,
and there are eggs: a miraculous
glut of color, truer than jewelry.

Let the world be made of silent
applause in the eyes of birds
as they gather and lurk.
Their pleasure is palpable; it smells
like easy money. How peaceful

it must be to find truth
in taxidermy, to side with these
birds and their sport-
fisherman with his prize.

To not think of that other
panicking
mind of dark water,
and of the minutes that slipped her,
astounded, to the end.

## Pinion

So it is true
that living makes you
lighter,

as if dying
had made you
a solid

thing I can hold
so painfully
close,

for a moment
I cease
being human.

Now that I've lived
to see you
vanish, I see

what you mean
is the same
as what you meant

living:
my windfall,
my luck entirely.

# Summer

1

As if to break my wrist,
or will,
she foots the glove—
makes me know
my bones. She is second
nature now, like riding a horse
at twelve, before my body
became my body.
At the first touch of air,
her wings rise—

the vise on my forearm
tightens;
her hackles are up—
three layers of leather
punctured and a small
cry like an animal's I realize
later is mine.

2

The horse I paid to ride
was nearly blind.
It was the last
summer of her life.
The trail, in August
air like old glass,
waved us forward. I wanted
to be a horse. I still don't know
what happened to her body.

No severing, no last
look in the eye.
All year vultures
rode their thermals.
One day I came for her
and she was gone.

# Eyas

Her hunger—part goblin,
part grief for the stink of the nest,
its feathers and filth, castings
of bone and fur. Then my hand
comes out of sky to her blindness,
palming her body
into its warmth. And her mouth
gapes open.

There is blood enough
to feed her and others
wait to be fed, but she
is the first I will see go from hand
to glove. She is not mine, yet
when the pulse in my finger meets
the pulse of her skull, I am mother
to strangeness. Beneath the sky's
field, my world pivots.

# Propagation

A vulture will kill for her eggs.
This one kills her own
chicks as they hatch, a captive's
perversity. She was not
born to this; she goes on
living unreleasably. We
give her wood eggs
to sit instead;
hers go under broody
cochin hens. They
do nothing but sit—
their heat the singular
gift of their bodies.
They would starve before
leaving the eggs.
It is what they were bred for,
their blood so tame I wonder
if there is any wildness left.
We, too, are in servitude
to vultures. They hiss
as we back from their nest.
They have a future
to protect. It is in my hand—
heavy, alive, a warm
globe breathing in its shell.

# Flown

The clouds are still gifts. My mornings are filled with them.
All this month of thickening sky, of blues
illumined, the color of weather,

I have asked too much.
I've held like stairs, treacherous
at night and in rainfall, gone on

making my joints fit
my body, my body fit
the world I've bled into.

I have always been bad at hanging on.
Even in this clearest of air
I beg let me be wing

without soul. Black eye fast in my feathers.

# Elegy

In everything
I see I try to fit her
body. Slender
stem of new
grass in winter,
I name you green
wing, lost
in amazement.
I have strayed
from the trail. In the cold
there is a silver
sound of leaves,
of animals calling.
The bluntness
of longing, the arc
of branches, new
buds like spines that catch
the wind and make
a song.
I call back and nothing
answers. Not she
who was so
small one leaf could
cover her. I want
to walk backward into spring—
last year's turtle, the elk
coming close to the road.
At the lake I turn
and see a ghost. She is me
seen-through, like the jar

I raise; my hand—
she scatters, lifted
like ash by a breeze.

# Iris

Dead, though I pick them anyway,
because they are mine.
Because their time is over
I let nothing grow, listen
to the ghosts of them,

each with her message
from Lethe. Each limp
stem in a bed of broken
necks a fallen bird. We've all

mistaken windowed sky
for heaven;—it is
always spring.
Stem. Leaf. Blossom.
All of it sponged from the air.

## Candling Eggs

At one end of the egg an owl—
her head, her wing stumps clear as fingers,
the black pulse of her heart
beating. In the dark
with only the egg-
glow, its tracery
of veins, its membrane,
I am trying to let go of you.
There is no ritual for raising
the dead. I see how it is—
the sky between us, threads
of sky, soft, pale-
blue flickering in silver
glints off the white
branches that spread, my
hand held up as if I
could stop your fall. It comes
to this—warm egg, my palm
made momentary cradle.
Then the wobbly
rise of her head, her fight
for breath, for flesh. For now,
only my eye enters the thin
scrim of her shell.
My eye that carries you with it,
like a flaw
in my iris the shape of a wing.

The last line of "King Vulture" was taken from J. A. Baker's *The Peregine.*

"Afterimage" was inspired by an exhibition entitled *The Villa of the Mysteries in Pompeii: Ancient Ritual, Modern Muse.* Fragments of text are taken from the catalogue.

Lone Elk Park, in Valley Park, Missouri, was named for the one surviving elk from a herd slaughtered by the U.S. military when the grounds became an ammunition storage and testing site during the Korean War. The original herd, transported from Yellowstone National Park in 1951, numbered two bulls and eight cows. By 1958, the year of their slaughter, they numbered over 100. In 1966, thanks in part to fundraising by local schools, five additional elk were brought to the park. Today the park grounds serve as a sanctuary for elk, bison, wolves, and birds of prey.

The italicized lines in "Brazil, 1832" were taken from *The Voyage of the Beagle* by Charles Darwin.

The final lines of "Riverlands" owe a debt to writer and falconer Stephen Bodio.

The title and inspiration for *"And he sang he would tear her to pieces"* is the Nigerian folktale "The Leopard Man."

## Iowa Poetry Prize and Edwin Ford Piper
## Poetry Award Winners

1987
Elton Glaser, *Tropical Depressions*
Michael Pettit, *Cardinal Points*

1988
Bill Knott, *Outremer*
Mary Ruefle, *The Adamant*

1989
Conrad Hilberry, *Sorting the Smoke*
Terese Svoboda, *Laughing Africa*

1990
Philip Dacey, *Night Shift at the Crucifix Factory*
Lynda Hull, *Star Ledger*

1991
Greg Pape, *Sunflower Facing the Sun*
Walter Pavlich, *Running near the End of the World*

1992
Lola Haskins, *Hunger*
Katherine Soniat, *A Shared Life*

1993
Tom Andrews, *The Hemophiliac's Motorcycle*

Michael Heffernan, *Love's Answer*
John Wood, *In Primary Light*

1994
James McKean, *Tree of Heaven*
Bin Ramke, *Massacre of the Innocents*
Ed Roberson, *Voices Cast Out to Talk Us In*

1995
Ralph Burns, *Swamp Candles*
Maureen Seaton, *Furious Cooking*

1996
Pamela Alexander, *Inland*
Gary Gildner, *The Bunker in the Parsley Fields*
John Wood, *The Gates of the Elect Kingdom*

1997
Brendan Galvin, *Hotel Malabar*
Leslie Ullman, *Slow Work through Sand*

1998
Kathleen Peirce, *The Oval Hour*
Bin Ramke, *Wake*
Cole Swensen, *Try*